children's room

essentials

JUDITH WILSON

children's room
essentials

RYLAND
PETERS
& SMALL
LONDON NEW YORK

Designer Emilie Ekström
Senior editor Henrietta Heald
Picture research Claire Hector
Production Deborah Wehner
Art director Gabriella Le Grazie
Publishing director Alison Starling

10 9 8 7 6 5 4 3 2 1

Some of the text in this book first
appeared in *Children's Spaces*.

First published in the United Kingdom
in 2004 by Ryland Peters & Small, Inc.
519 Broadway
New York, NY 10012
London W1T 2RP
www.rylandpeters.com

Text copyright © Judith Wilson 2004
Design and photographs copyright
© Ryland Peters & Small 2004

Library of Congress Cataloging-in-Publication Data

Wilson, Judith, 1962-
  Children's room essentials / Judith Wilson.
    p. cm.
  ISBN 1-84172-685-0
  1. Children's rooms. 2. Interior decoration. I. Title.
  NK2117.C4W55 2004
  747.7'7'083--dc22
                                    2004004910

Printed and bound in China.

12/06

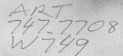

contents

bedroom

styles

Right This nursery storage unit was specially built by a carpenter. The cupboard has a pull-out changing surface and a box to hold baby wipes, plus shelves for diapers.
Opposite If you combine proper cupboard storage with easy-access shelves, toddlers can easily reach their favorite things.
Below Scaled-down furniture is a friendly as well as a practical part of a toddler's bedroom.

babies' rooms

A baby needs little in the early days, although department stores might try to persuade you otherwise. Many infants don't even move into their own rooms until three months or beyond, perfectly content to swing in a cradle at their parents' bedside. Nevertheless, a new arrival does need its own bedroom, for diaper changing, storing clothes, and to house a nascent collection of toys.

The main nursery basic is a crib. Simple styles are both practical and chic. More enticing than traditional varnished pine are beech or cherrywood, white-painted wood, colorful melamine, or ironwork. A baby bed, with slatted sides that are removed as the baby grows up, is a cost-effective option.

A padded bumper protects restless little heads, but choose one in plain colors and with quilting, not ruffles. Cotton sheets and blankets and a comforting quilt are the other basics. When your baby is two years old, add a baby pillow. Blankets and sheets are now available in every color. Pick and choose between different coordinated lines, or add a retro piece or two.

The area for changing diapers should be efficient and fuss-free. Don't bother to buy a special unit, which will soon be redundant. A chest of drawers at the correct height, with a plastic padded mat on top, can double as a changing area. Store all the essentials—diapers, wipes, and creams—in drawers immediately below, or place them on a chunky shelf above the chest yet still within arm's reach. If you have room, consider a custommade unit. You will need alcoves for clothes, cotton balls, diapers, and so on, with a pull-out or pull-down changing surface.

A low, comfortable armchair is a must for feeding. Get a slip cover made in a sturdy, washable fabric—bright denim, robust linen, or terrycloth. If there's room, beanbags in jelly-bean colors or wipe-clean vinyl cubes are great for babies learning to sit up or crawl.

White walls and a neutral floor make the ideal backdrop for colorful accessories. But if you (and your baby) need stimulation, paint one wall a bold shade such as cherry red or swimming-pool turquoise. If you prefer soothing pastels, stronger tones such as lavender or duck's-egg blue make the best background for primary-colored toys. Try painting abstract shapes: stripes or giant dots look good. Don't forget the ceiling—babies spend hours on their backs.

String the ceiling with Chinese lanterns, party bunting, or paper mobiles. You don't have to cover the walls with pictures, but you and baby need something lovely to look at.

Opposite, left Simple embroidery can be used to give baby sheets or pillowcases a personal touch.
Opposite, right Take advantage of natural light by putting a crib under a window, but make sure that you have a blind or curtain that is efficient enough to exclude glare.
Below and left In a baby girl's nursery, a whitewashed antique crib sets the tone for a simple yet pretty room. Pastel-painted pegs hung with tiny dresses brighten white walls, and an ever-changing display of nostalgic pictures, family snapshots, and paintings means that there is always something stimulating for the baby to look at.

Above Bright colors and abstract shapes make a baby's room more stimulating. The low armchair is a comfortable place for feeding.
Above right The double divan with surround on a tubular frame is ideal for a toddler who has outgrown a crib but is not yet ready for a bed.
Opposite Not all babies have the luxury of their own room. A crib in a corner of the parents' bedroom can be individualized in small decorative ways, with lengths of colorful bunting, for example.

Use imaginative lighting to add a creative dimension. If there's an overhead light, install a dimmer switch, essential for checking on the baby at night. Plunder both adult and children's lighting departments for unusual options. In addition to "magic lantern" children's lamps, which splash the walls with gentle color and movement, consider a lava lamp, strings of flower fairy lights, illuminated globes, or punched-metal lampshades that cast patterns.

You'll probably need more space for baby clothes than you expect. Little shirts and sleepsuits make quite a pile, then there are gifts of clothes waiting to be worn, as well as outgrown garments. A closet isn't essential. Instead, choose a generous chest with plenty of drawers, which can be updated with a coat of paint or contemporary handles. A giant laundry basket is a must for a fast turnover of clothes. Wicker baskets, zinc tubs, or colorful plastic crates stacked on shelves or tucked beneath the crib will all make clearing up easy.

- Plain **painted** walls create the most **restful** ambience in a baby's **first** room.

- Keep things simple with **clear** colors, **quick-access** storage, and a stimulating view from **the crib**.

- Sensory touches add **magic**—perhaps a **wind chime** or twinkling mini lights.

- Anticipate the **crawling** phase by keeping blind cords short, trailing cables clipped, and **plug covers** on.

Far left A swathe of fabric with a slot heading adds sophistication to a simple metal bed frame.
Left This painted lampstand has a decorative as well as a practical function, combining fun and order.
Below left The striking lime walls, purple rubber flooring, and scarlet spotty-dotty bedcover are very appealing to young taste.
Opposite Built-in storage does not have to mean cupboards. The high platform bed in this teenager's bedroom incorporates plenty of large drawers. The wall-mounted TV shelf also saves on floor space.

girls' rooms

Most little girls love pretty things. But give your daughter a break from the classic flowery bedroom and offer her instead a fresh, contemporary take on the feminine look. Crisp pastel colors or an all-white room make the perfect background for little girls to display their special treasures. For tomboys, more subdued shades and quirky, abstract patterns are appealing.

Below right A Victorian day bed, with decorative open ironwork, makes an attractive bed choice for older girls. It looks particularly romantic draped with a fabric canopy or mosquito net.

Below Girls love to admire their clothes, so provide space to line up shoes, plus low hooks for hanging up hats and party dresses.

When a toddler turns two and graduates from a crib to a bed, it provides a timely moment for reassessing the bedroom and making stylistic changes. Focus first on the hard-working furniture, planning colors later. Invest in the best mattress you can afford. Children may be light, but they need firm support, and a good-quality mattress should last for ten years. Think long and hard about the style of bed you choose. Girls will go through myriad fads, from Barbie-doll fever at five to seriously sophisticated at ten. Work backwards. If a classic style with a contemporary twist seems suitable for a preteen, it can be made appropriately childlike for the earlier years.

Canopied and four-poster beds, bunk beds, or sleeping platforms prove irresistible to girls, as well as providing extra space for sleepover friends. A simple wood or tubular metal four-poster offers plenty of decorative potential. Frames can be draped with brightly colored net one year, homemade strings of shells the next, or with inexpensive, glittery sari silks for older girls. A platform bed can usefully accommodate storage or a desk beneath, and for stylistic continuity can be custommade in materials used elsewhere in the house. Practical plywood, melamine, or galvanized steel are all options, and will be softened with colorful bed linen and teddies. Just as little girls love to choose their dolls' clothes,

Above and above left A metal bedstead is a good investment, since it can be restyled from year to year or resprayed in a different color. Hunt down antique ones in secondhand stores. A headboard at each end has its advantages, providing somewhere to pile up pillows and to hang bags and toys. An older girl will appreciate lots of open storage. Here, school books, toys, and treasures are all at hand.

they'll relish the chance to mix and match pillowcases and bedspreads. Provided they are from a complementary palette, crisp checks, solids, and florals mixed with white will look great jumbled together on the bed. Extras such as an embroidered pillowcase, cozy travel blanket, or appliquéd top sheet make the final effect more individual.

The bed may be a top priority, but storage comes a close second. Plan for, or with, your daughter by writing a list of everything she needs to keep in her bedroom, from toys and clothes to decorative inessentials. Not everything has to be put away at all times, but each item should have a home.

If the room is large enough, the smartest and simplest storage option is to put in a closet with floor-to-ceiling, flush-fitting doors along one wall. Behind this façade you should provide a multitude of different-sized shelves,

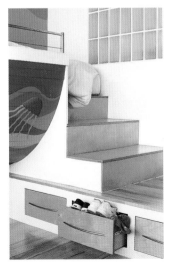

roomy enough to hold individual crates for small items yet deep enough for piles of sweaters and jeans, and including space for a clothesrod. Open shelves may seem a tempting option for finding toys at a glance, but closed doors look neater.

Ideally, you should provide an area for your little girl to draw and do her homework. Take a tip from contemporary interiors and provide her with a long, low work surface with wall-mounted shelves above. It could be painted wood or covered in stainless steel or colorful laminate. Site the computer here; beneath the bench, fit crates on castors for toys or books, a second stool for a friend,

Above Create a dramy, tranquil atmosphere with pretty lighting such as paper globes, Chinese lanterns, or a mini chandelier.
Above left Young sisters may prefer sharing a low double bed with two quilts rather than having single beds at opposite ends of the room.
Left Don't assume girls want a fairy grotto. This little girl's bed, with its seafaring theme, has delighted her since her toddler years.
Opposite A custom-made platform bed in painted plywood is a brilliant space saver as well as creating a cozy, self-contained unit.

even a cabinet with lots of shallow drawers for coloring pens and paper. If you add a mirror, a countertop can also double as a dressing table and display space.

Most children relish a colorful environment and will want to be involved in choosing their favorite shades. Follow the same rules as you would anywhere else in the house. Jolly brights like sherbet yellow or cornflower blue are stimulating, but use them on a single wall so the effect isn't overpowering.

Remember that your daughter's room is her private haven, a place for chats with friends, somewhere quiet to do homework, a retreat for dreaming and scheming. Help her to delineate her territory from other siblings so she can be alone when she chooses. You could mark her door with a giant gilded initial, for example, or get a metalwork company to cut out her name in stainless-steel letters.

Left Nothing beats open cube shelves for quick toy storage. Fit some with doors so that messier items can be concealed.
Right Include scaled-down pieces, such as tiny chairs. Pick light, easy-to-move designs, so that girls can rearrange them during play.
Above right Mini totes provide impromptu storage.
Opposite Children enjoy the cozy sloping ceilings of an attic room, but it can be hard to squeeze in conventional furniture. Commission a carpenter to custom-build shelves and cupboards under the eaves.

- Painted walls rather than **wallpaper**, display space for treasured **accessories**, and classic furniture all make for a **relaxed**, easy bedroom.

- Just as little girls love to choose their **dolls' clothes**, they'll relish the chance to **mix and match** pillowcases and bedspread colors.

- For a girl who likes privacy, create a **hideaway**. String suspension wire between walls to **divide off** the bed area, and add a voile curtain.

- Little girls love to display **treasures**, so provide a good, generous shelf or table top for all those **papier-mâché** models, beach shells, sparkly **tiaras,** and family photos.

boys' rooms

Boys care passionately about their bedrooms. From around the age of six, most of them know instinctively what accessories and motifs are "cool" and will want to incorporate at least some into their private space. They may fuss less than girls about an overall scheme, but are obsessive when it comes to the smaller details. What boys need most is empty floor space—as much as you can spare—and plenty of storage so that their myriad collections, from toy soldiers to racing cars, can stay well ordered and ready for play.

Left A bunk bed is an excellent option for a boy's room. Your son can sleep on the safe lower level until about age six, and graduate to the higher level when he feels ready for it.

Above and opposite Choose quirky, vibrant colors for a bright, trendy boy's room. Wall-mount as much furniture as possible, leaving space for all the essentials of the boy zone—a football table, dartboard, punchbag, or basketball hoop.

Everything in a boy's room should be robust. Imagine each piece of furniture being jumped off, climbed on, or moved around as part of a pirate ship game or impromptu pillow fight, and you'll get a realistic picture. Pick scratch-resistant modern materials like laminate and plywood, or painted furniture that can be easily touched up with a lick of paint.

Boys still require a cozy sleeping nook at the age of three, but by five are ready for a more adventurous, classically boyish option. Either buy a generously sized crib for the baby stage and get a serious boy's bed once your son outgrows the crib or invest in a grown-up bed at the age of two, and make it inviting for the early years.

Boys, as much as girls, appreciate a fuss being made over their bed. It does not simply represent somewhere to sleep, but is a child's special secure zone as well as being a potential platform for imaginative games. Ready-to-buy modern options might include sophisticated dark wood or painted bateau-lit and sleigh-bed frames, simple iron bedsteads, or colorful melamine platform beds with storage drawers. For most boys past the age of five, a bunk bed is a dream option. A number of stores now stock tubular metal bunk beds, which are infinitely more stylish than the varnished-pine variety.

A platform bed frees up more floor space for playing, so it is a boon in a small room. Storage cupboards, a generous run of

Left In this toddler's bedroom, a high picket-fence headboard, a faux-fur rug, and thick, tufted curtains promote a safe, cozy feel.
Below Furniture on castors and bright plastic storage crates that can be slotted under the bed are invaluable in a small room.
Opposite, left As an alternative to dog-eared posters, consider a bold painted canvas depicting your son's favorite sports hero.
Opposite, right Brilliant, saturated color on every surface, from walls to furniture, transforms an ordinary bedroom into an entertaining playroom. Here, the startling walls are matched by equally vibrant bed linen—a riot of crazy stripes, animals, and exotic fruit.

work surface or, with a lower bed, lots of pull-out drawers, can be variously incorporated underneath. Make furniture on castors a theme—everything from a chest of drawers to a low play table. Even better, clear the floor with wall-mounted shelves for books, baskets for miscellaneous bits and pieces, hooks for clothes, and even ceiling-suspended seating— perhaps a hammock or a swinging pod chair.

Most boys have little interest in putting clothes away, so devise a simple storage system. Open shelves in a closet are the easiest option, but clearly label each section for T-shirts, jeans, and so on. Alternatively, build a series of box-shaped cupboards at child height all around the room, with each one

devoted to a certain category of clothing, and equipped with a different-colored door to resemble a school locker. Give your son a row of child-height hooks where he can hang his pajamas or anything else that has been strewn across the floor. Don't expect him to line up his shoes neatly. Instead, provide one big basket, and agree that this is the designated place for all shoes at clearing-up time.

Little boys play constantly on the floor, so flooring should be hard-wearing and attractive as well as providing a smooth surface. There's nothing more frustrating than trying to race

Below left A custom-built bed maximizes space in a small room, and adds quirky charm. And little children are less likely to fall out of beds that are boxed in or have high sides. Storage can be incorporated in the form of under-bed drawers.

Below and opposite page Detailing counts for just as much in a child's bedroom as it does in a grown-up space. Ornaments should be fun and colorful, and boys should have plenty of space to show off treasures. A shelf unit can be the decorative centerpiece of a room, and it needn't always be spotlessly neat. Children love anything that spells out their name. Letters on the door lend an air of importance, as does anything monogrammed.

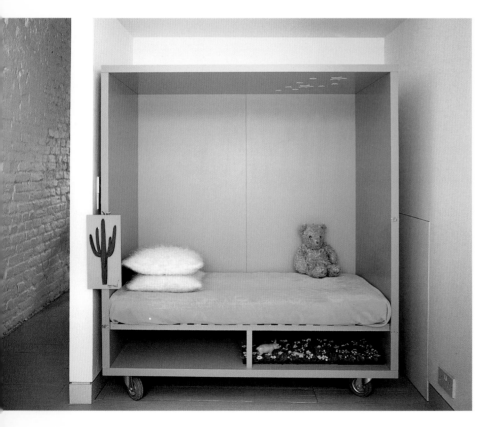

cars along badly sanded wooden boards, or to arrange army platoons on bumpy sisal matting. Far more practical, and infinitely more stylish, are painted or waxed wooden boards, wood laminate flooring, or brightly colored rubber tiles.

If your son is crazy about a cartoon character, indulge his passion with a giant floor cushion made in appropriate fabric or a big poster, then ignore further demands. Crazes come and go, and next year he will have moved on to another phase. If you create a neutral canvas with plain painted walls and a white roll-up shade, you can introduce any theme.

Boys may be boisterous and busy, but there are times when they want a special area in their bedroom for relaxing and being with friends. If there's no room for a sofa, give your little

Right Low hooks provide quick access to clothes. Look for decorative, themed designs, but make sure pegs are long enough to hold clothes securely.

Below Built-in storage and a bed all along one wall free up play space. With bedding stored in big drawers beneath it, the bed can be used for somersaults or sitting with friends.

Opposite Mixed with simple wooden furniture, a collection of old-fashioned toys creates a nostalgic bedroom. Use one piece to inspire a decorative theme: mix a sailing boat with nautical stripes, or tin soldiers with camouflage motifs.

boy the chance to turn his bed into a lounge-lizard spot. He will enjoy touchy-feely fabrics on the bed. Choose bedspreads and sheets in strong solids and add a pure-wool checked blanket. A giant fleece-fabric blanket in a vivid hue such as scarlet or grass green looks neat tucked over the blanket by day. A cut-up old sleeping bag, made into squishy cushions, is also fun. Give boys a chance to create their own ambience in the room using lighting—a bubble lamp by the bed, a light-up globe on the desk, or a funky coil of lights are all good options. Try to squeeze in a few quirky additions. A football table, punchbag, or wall-hung basketball hoop will make your son's room the coolest den he could ask for.

• For boys, aim to create a **cool den** that's fuss-free and has versatile **furniture** for **imaginative** play.

• Raid the **color spectrum** for inspiration—scarlet, leaf green, **indigo**—then team with robust surfaces such as **rubber** and **wood**.

• For toys, the **ideal** storage system combines plenty of **small drawers**, crates, or boxes with **bookshelves**.

• A **steel** pinboard, equipped with magnets, is a great place to display **school art work** and certificates.

shared rooms

Plenty of children share a bedroom. As a parent, you may anticipate only the downside of this arrangement: disrupted bedtimes, arguments over territory, one child wanting to study while the other chooses to chat. But it needn't be a nightmare. Ask any grown-up who shared a room to recall childhood memories, and many will remember the fun of reading by flashlight after lights-out or the pleasure of two sets of toys. Besides, for a child to wake up with his or her siblings and fall asleep with them each night is a great gift.

Left and opposite One way to approach a room shared by a boy and a girl is to keep the basic units unisex. Here, polished boards, metal cupboards, and metal-legged beds provide a neutral background. Give each child's area a distinct character by using the bed and wall behind it as a focal point.

Below This room for older boys takes a shared dormitory as its theme. White shutters, plain floorboards, and utilitarian metal-framed beds all suggest summer camp, while the furniture—a battered locker, individual initialed trunks, and aluminum chairs—completes the look.

Children sharing a bedroom will find it fun to have a formal division of territory, so that during arguments or when entertaining friends each can retreat to their private zone. First, decide if the division will be visual or physical. For little ones, the less physical separation the better. They will derive comfort at night by having their beds close together, and reading a joint story will be simpler for you.

If your children get along well, divide the room space into separate sleeping, play, and work zones instead of two distinct areas with bed, chest, and so on. Bunk beds or sleeping pods on a shared platform can be divided from the play space with a sliding screen or curtains. The children can either share one long countertop to do homework or have two identical desks side by side.

When a boy and a girl share, you will need to reconcile two definite and differing tastes. For little ones, paint walls white or choose a bold shade, then personalize each child's bed. There's nothing more charming than two identical bedsteads side by side, but characterize each with different bedspreads: an identical design, perhaps, but in two contrasting colors. Take the theme a step further, and color-coordinate each child's bedside table, rug, and lampshade.

When same-sex siblings are sharing, you can easily indulge all-girl fantasies or all-boy passions. But you still need to personalize the two-of-everything accessories, so that sharers are clear about who owns what.

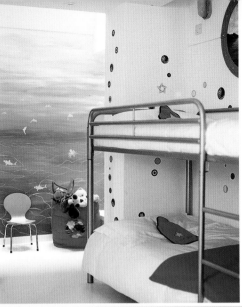

Far left Two divans placed at right angles, with a shared, sturdy cube side table, is a comforting and sensible option for small children.
Left and below Bunk-bed styles, in minimal tubular steel or ready-to-paint wood or are ideal for a shared room, and perennial favorites with children, perhaps because they double as climbing frames. If there is a playroom elsewhere in your house, a shared room can be kept ultra-simple.

Some children are messy, while others are neat, so to avoid arguments over clearing up give each child his or her own chest of drawers, shelves, or closet. A bedside table for each, to hold a nighttime drink, books, and lamp, is also essential. Since shared rooms frequently double as playrooms, make sure that everything can be cleared away quickly and hidden behind closed doors.

If you have picked a stimulating decorative scheme, flexible lighting is one way to calm things down at bedtime. In shared rooms, the right lighting is especially important. Different-aged children may have staggered lights-out times, so that while an older child needs a task light for reading in bed, a younger sibling might need a glowing nightlight. For playtime, low-voltage ceiling lights provide brighter illumination than a single overhead pendant, but equip them with a dimmer switch.

Above right One way to resolve the issue of kids with differing tastes is with a dominant mural, which can negate the need for boundaries. It makes the room that contains it everyone's room—a magical place to go to sleep and wake up.
Right Each child needs somewhere to keep special toys. Provide a "secret" box for under the bed, or agree that toys placed on a certain chair must not be touched.
Opposite In this shared all-girls room, the symmetry of side-by-side sleigh beds and twin chairs creates a tranquil ambience.

When children enjoy sharing a bedroom, it becomes a real den, their own private space versus the family house. If space permits, give them a daybed or an inflatable chair to lounge on, and consider installing a TV for older kids. If there is a younger sibling who doesn't share, and everyone is in agreement, the daybed could be used at weekends for sleepovers so the little one can join in the fun. Likewise, give each child who shares the chance to sleep alone occasionally, in a spare bedroom or on the sofabed. Children, like adults, need some time away from the fray.

- Siblings who share need clearly marked **personal zones**, their own private corners, and **decoration** that they both **adore**.

- **Give** the room two of everything, then create a **fun environment** that's ideal for shared play and midnight **snacks**, yet serene enough for soothing bedtimes.

- A colorful **fantasy mural** will appeal to both sexes, but try to keep shapes **simple** and the look graphic.

a bedroom is ...

Children, just like **adults**, need privacy, so give them **freedom** to enjoy **time out** in their **individual** bedrooms.

Kids will like being **involved** in a room scheme they can be **proud of**—and will be more likely to keep the room **neat**.

a child's private space

Plan bedrooms that are fun for **little friends**, with seating to chill out on, or a futon for **sleepovers**.

Adopt a five-year plan, and anticipate each **new** need, from a work desk to **funky furnishings** for preteens.

living

spaces

play spaces

Every child needs space to play. An expanse of floor, a freshly cleared tabletop, and enough room to race around are the essentials. As adults, we allocate ourselves activity zones—a sofa to sprawl on, a desk for paying bills—and children need their own equivalent. Size should not be the issue; whether it's a patch of floor in a kitchen or dining room, or a separate playroom, what's important is that this is an area that children can call their own. If you make toys accessible and easy to put away, your kids will even enjoy organizing their own private zone.

Opposite, left A wooden desktop, fixed on an adjustable rack system, provides a corner for quiet play or drawing and writing.

Opposite, right Experiment with shelving levels, especially in a small space. Shelves can be run around a room at ceiling height, hung below a window, or wall-mounted.

Left Tall shelving units can serve kids' and adults' needs alike. Dangerous or precious items, or infrequently used toys and books, can be stored well out of the way while lower shelves are devoted to everyday necessities.

Below Look for gadgets that keep play equipment neat inside a cupboard: stacking boxes, plastic CD racks, and a wooden paper dispenser are all good options.

Above Don't feel obliged to keep everything small—the best dens will appeal to adults, too. Choose squashy beanbags, a wall-size blackboard, or a big chill-out sofa.
Opposite, left A low custommade bench, teamed with a freestanding play table and chairs, makes a cozy place for adults and children in the playroom. Design one with a lift-up lid, so there is more storage inside.
Opposite, right In a large playroom, try to incorporate desk space for older children, for doing homework or using a family computer.

There are many advantages to an open-plan living space. Tiny children can play safely under a grown-up's watchful eye while cooking, watching a video or DVD, and older kids' homework all get under way. If you are moving home to accommodate a growing family, this is the ideal space configuration to aim for. It is helpful to have a bathroom nearby, so little ones don't have to travel too far from their toys. And, if possible, access from the living area/play space to a yard or safe roof terrace is invaluable.

If you can't move but are adapting your living quarters to suit children, think long and hard about the changes you make. You will reap the benefits of employing an architect, although it may seem expensive at the time. An architect will think laterally about maximizing space and can squeeze storage into the most unlikely corners. Alternatively, if finances are tight, can rooms be swapped around? Perhaps a dining room off the kitchen could be made into a playroom? But if you have a spare room away from the living area that might be converted into a separate playroom, think twice about doing so when your children are small. You don't want to be cooking with half an ear on what's going on next door, and life is easier if you don't have to call a halt to exciting play in one room and move children to the kitchen to eat.

The disadvantage of sharing a space with kids is that they bring a sea of bright plastic with them. Provide effective storage so that toys can be put away quickly and grown-up order restored. One solution is to equip the space with floor-to-ceiling cupboards with flush doors and deep shelves. Put kids' things on the lower shelves and household items on the upper ones. If you can, specify extra-deep cupboards so that fold-up doll buggies or plastic garages can fit in easily. If open shelves are the only option, invest in containers that look good en masse.

Precious or beautiful pieces should be put into storage or placed firmly out of reach. If you have the luxury of a grown-ups-only living room, enjoy them there. It's easy to teach children to respect lovely things and not to draw on the walls, but sensible to accept that accidents will happen. So protect your cherrywood dining table with a wipe-clean vinyl cloth and your expensively upholstered sofa with a slipcover made from tough washable fabric. Replace a limited-edition rug with an abstract one from a chain store. Beaded cushions, velvet throws, or anything else labeled "dry clean only" should be removed. Remember, you are creating a child-friendly zone so that everyone can relax.

The beauty of integrating kids' stuff with contemporary design is that trendy industrial-style surfaces like stainless steel, plywood, and laminate are stylish and hard-wearing, and the clear, bright colors of much modern furniture are enhanced when littered with toys. Walls painted in white flat vinyl latex create a simple background, but you can have fun with color, too. A single wall in dazzling bright blue can look stunning, particularly if decorated with children's artwork.

Polypropylene chairs are a practical, easy-clean option, and 1960s-style versions in vivid tangerine or lime green are great fun. If a table doubles as a dining and painting table, a wipe-clean surface is essential, so a laminated top is perfect. To house a video or DVD machine, choose a long cabinet rather than open shelves. Have a steel one powder-coated in pink, and make a design statement

at the same time. You can also be imaginative when selecting fabric for the playroom sofa or chairs. Several bright solids can create an abstract effect if used as blocks of color on individual chairs, seats, and cushions. Patterned fabric is good for disguising sticky finger marks. When decorating a play space, you can be a little tongue-in-cheek. A 1970s swivel chair upholstered in Bob the Builder fabric would look suitably funky, as might a giant abstract painting that blurs the barriers between modern art and kids' naïve efforts.

Every play area should have a cozy corner for watching a video or DVD, or listening to music. If space permits, a small sofa is wonderful for after-lunch naps or quiet reading; if there is not enough room for this, beanbags work equally well. Play spaces in communal living areas often have hard floors, perhaps wood or limestone, so a rug or a fluffy faux animal-print throw provides a softer sitting or crawling area for babies and toddlers.

Above A freestanding, floor-level bookshelf is ideal for small children, making books simple to stack.
Above left Shallow drawers are excellent for organizing pens, paper, and art materials. Look for a play table with an integral drawer, or plastic drawer units on wheels.
Opposite, left The best storage is both practical and good-looking.
Opposite, right Deep drawers hold plenty of toys and are easy for children to reach. Be imaginative with the drawer fronts: cut out patterns from wood or choose stainless-steel or wooden fascias.

play spaces should allow ...

Modern **flooring** materials such as concrete make the **perfect** surfaces for toy trains and cars.

Every **play space** needs comfortable low-level seating for relaxing in front of a video or **reading**.

the imagination to roam

Put art equipment and **materials** in low cupboards or **on open shelves**, so kids can have **easy access** to them.

Stainless steel, wood, **laminate**, and painted board offer **hard-wearing** play surfaces that **clean up** efficiently.

eating spaces

Children's mealtimes may resemble lunchtime at the zoo, but if you choose practical equipment and furniture at least it shouldn't take long to clean up. Babies progress rapidly from being spoon-fed to helping themselves in a highchair and then graduating to the grown-ups' table. Whatever stage your children have reached, the process of getting them to sit down, eat calmly, and observe table manners needs to be achieved with minimum fuss and maximum efficiency.

Opposite, left Miniature table and chair sets need not be clumsy pieces of molded plastic in garish colors. For an individual and stylish look, choose more elegant versions that mimic grown-up contemporary classic styles.

Opposite, right In a large multifunctional kitchen, plan to retain a generous area of floor space, so that small children have plenty of room to run around—then group together the activity zones for intimacy and practicality. Children like perching on chairs close enough to chat to parents while they prepare food.

Left and below In a corridor-style kitchen, even the smallest table makes the room user-friendly for children.

If possible, put a children's dining table in the kitchen, so you can keep an eye on the kids while preparing food or clearing up. Don't despair that your high-tech contemporary kitchen will be spoiled by highchairs and brightly colored dishes. Colorful seating, a lime-green toaster, or pink plastic beakers will only pep up the stainless-steel cabinets.

A highchair is essential for babies. Standard designs are practical, but can be an eyesore. Better-looking ones include simple wooden Scandinavian designs or plain white lacquered steel versions. Or look for a secondhand highchair, repaint it in a bold color, and re-cover the seat in a retro-print oilcloth. A sturdy canvas or plastic clip-on seat is sociable for older babies, because it fixes onto the tabletop.

Little ones often like to have a diminutive table and chairs at which they can eat meals or draw and paint. But, if you like to sit with the kids while they eat, you may not find it very comfortable. Eating at a breakfast bar or adding a low countertop to the end of an island unit might be a better solution. The sooner you encourage small children to sit up at the adults' table, the better, but if you have a beautiful table, protect it with a vinyl cloth at all times.

Polypropylene, metal, or wood chairs are good for family mealtimes. Pick a style that is comfortable and safe for children as well as looking smart. School-style benches are also excellent, offering extra room for friends.

Left The combination of a breakfast zone on a counter and a separate dining table means that homework or drawing needn't be cleared away when meals are served.
Below If planning a kitchen/dining room from scratch, choose units with children's needs in mind. This kitchen looks slick, but is in bright, fun shades. Storage for tableware has been cleverly combined with shelves for art materials and books.
Opposite An island unit makes the ideal breakfast bar for slightly older children: a 10 inch (25 cm) overhang on the counter gives adequate leg-room. Furnish it with high stools, which children love.

With imaginative shopping, you and the children will find laying the table positively creative. Tiny versions of anything will delight them, and a choice of colors is great, because each can pick his or her favorite. Not everything has to be plastic, though dayglo picnic sets are a good source of plates and cups. Duralex glass tumblers are virtually indestructible and come in appealingly small sizes. Many casual dining sets are made from robust pottery, and traditional enamel plates and cups are also hard-wearing.

Everything to do with children's mealtimes should be accessible for them, since it encourages setting the table from an early age. Store bowls and flatware in a low cupboard and drawers, and keep lunchboxes in there, too. Is the fridge easy for an older child to open, so they can help themselves to snacks? Is there a sturdy stool for a little one to hop onto so he can get a drink of water from the sink? The easier you make eating and drinking for your children, the sooner they will be integrated into the sociable world of family mealtimes.

make meals fun ...

Choose wipe-clean **furniture** and scaled-down shapes, with tableware in **jelly-bean** shades.

Give little ones a diminutive **table** and chairs at which they can eat meals or **draw** and paint.

Mix and match **tableware** to make meals more lively. Add jolly **accessories**, from funky flatware to a retro, tomato-shaped **ketchup dispenser**.

Pick **robust**, easy-mop flooring: laminate, **sanded** and painted wooden boards, vinyl, bright rubber, and **limestone** are all **practical** choices.

with vibrant eating spaces

bathrooms

The bathroom is one of the most hard-working spaces in the home. It must be efficient enough for the before-school wash and brush-up yet cozy enough to prompt fun-filled bathtimes. Most children have a love–hate relationship with their daily ablutions. One week, they will obsessively brush their teeth; the next, they are frightened of the shower. But nearly all little ones find it soothing to wallow in a bath.

Left If space allows, double sinks make perfect sense in a shared bathroom. Allocate one basin to the children, with a shelf for novelty soaps and toothbrushes. Provide steps so that little ones can stand at the right height.

Right Bathtime is much more fun for children if the bathroom has decorative touches that appeal to their imagination, such as these low shelves for bubble bath and toys.

Opposite Sealed or painted wooden boards are suitable for a children's bathroom, but wood laminates are sensitive to deluges of bath water.

When planning a bathroom from scratch, first decide whether to have a bathtub and separate shower cubicle or a shower attachment wall-mounted over the tub. Little ones generally prefer baths to showers, but may slip if they shower standing up in the tub. If an over-tub shower is the only option, buy a non-slip rubber mat and a groovy plastic shower curtain.

To cope with the early morning rush, two (or even three) sinks make sense. There are plenty of stylish, practical choices that are ideal for kids. Small stainless-steel bowls set into a stone or wood countertop look ultra-trendy, as do wall-hung white ceramic butler's sinks. A small basin designed for cloakroom use is another option.

Cross-head or lever faucets are much easier to handle than slippery, minimal round knobs, while a mixer tap will guard against hot scalds. A counter with inset sink provides ample space for washroom essentials. But if the sink is freestanding, set the toothbrush rack into a wall-mounted holder, so it can't be knocked over, and replace slippery soap bars with liquid soap in a neat chrome dispenser. A wall-hung toilet can be sited slightly lower than usual. Consider whether a push-button flush mechanism would be better than a stiff handle.

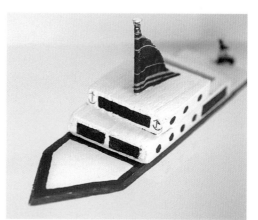

Left Rolltop bathtubs are good for children, since they have no sharp edges. Reconditioned Victorian ones often come in small sizes.
Below Efficient storage is essential in a shared bathroom. This one has under-sink cupboards as well as out-of-reach units for adult use.
Opposite page Kitsch plastic items such as bright fish, toy boats, and rubber dinosaurs make a children's bathroom more fun. Add a narrow shelf above the bath for display, or group objects along a windowsill.

If you make your bathroom 100 percent splashproof now, you won't mind about water fights later. Fun floor options include nonslip rubber tiles in bright colors, linoleum, or vinyl. Cork floor tiles with laminate finish also come in water-themed designs such as sand and shells. Sealed or painted wooden boards are also suitable. Stone, such as limestone or slate, is stylish and waterproof, but it gets slippery when wet, so invest in an absorbent bath mat.

Floor-to-ceiling tiles are a sensible idea for the walls. In a children-only bathroom, big, square tiles in a cheerful shade look graphic and modern. For a coordinated look, color-match them with laminate counters or a painted wooden floor. Walls can also be lined with tongue-and-groove or laminated panels. Paint them and the walls with eggshell, which resists condensation and splash marks. If sanitaryware is white, have fun with color on the walls. Jazzy shades such as grass green and turquoise are particularly appropriate.

Plan a **family** bathroom that is sophisticated enough for adults but **suitable** for **children**, too.

Surfaces must be **robust** and easy to clean. Vividly hued laminates make good **panels** and surrounds, while stone, from slate to **limestone**, is practical and **stylish**.

make your kids' bathroom ...

Plan plenty of storage for bathroom **paraphernalia**, including a high **lockable cabinet** for any medicines.

Provide a big **plastic bin** so that toys can be put away **easily** after bathtime.

a tempting place to be

resources

BEDS

The Bedroom Specialists
32526 Dahlstom Avenue
Abbotsford, B.C. V2T 6N2
Canada
604 859 2030
Children's beds.

Blackwelders
Call 800 438 0201 or visit
www.homefurnish.com/
blackwelders for a retailer
near you.
Bunk beds, sleigh beds.

buybuyBABY
1683 Rockville Pike
Rockville, MD 20852
301 984 1122
www.buybuybaby.com
Cribs, cradles, and bassinets.

FURNITURE

Ethan Allen Kids
3437 Wrightsboro Road
Augusta, GA 30909
706 737 9002
www.ethanallen.com
Furniture and bedroom
accessories.

For Mercy's Sake
3911 Kandy Drive
Austin, TX 78749
512 892 2077
Children's furniture.

Fun Time Designs Inc.
#375–2600 Granville Street
Vancouver, B.C. V6H 3V3
Canada
800 977 3443
Furniture featuring kids' favorite
cartoon characters.

Little Colorado
4450 Lipan Street
Denver, CO 80211
303 964 3212
Children's furniture.

My Second Step
2605 Lissa Jon Court
Raleigh, NC 27614
919 844 2293
Personalized children's
stepstools.

Tuffyland
H. Wilson Co.
555 West Taft Drive
South Holland, IL 60473
800 245 7224
www.tuffyland.com
Children's tables and chairs,
plus computer workstations.

Wildzoo Furniture
63025 O.B. Riley Road #9
Bend, OR 97701
888 543 8588
Children's furniture.

Workbench
470 Park Avenue
New York, NY 10016
212 481 5454
Children's furniture.

STORAGE

Frick and Frack's Toy Storage
1470 Route 23 North
Wayne, NJ 07470
973 696 6701
www.frickandfrack.com
Toy benches and children's
trunks.

Hold Everything
P.O. Box 7807
San Francisco, CA 94120
800 840 3596
www.holdeverything.com
Everything for storage from
baskets to shoe holders.

IKEA
Call 800 254 IKEA or visit
www.ikea.com for a retailer
near you.
Storage, furniture, and
accessories.

Inside Out Productions
10836 Washington Boulevard
Culver City, CA 90232
310 838 0255
www.insideoutproductions.com
Children's storage chairs.

BED LINEN

Babies "R" Us
Call 800BABY RUS or visit
www.babiesrus.com for a retailer
near you.
Complete line of linens for
babies.

Night and Day
7033 E 1st Avenue
Scottsdale, AZ 85251
480 481 5106
Babies' and children's linens,
decorative pillows, and robes.

Wamsutta
Springs Industries Inc.
P.O. Box 70
Fort Mill, SC 29716
800 831 1488
www.wamsutta.com
Pokémon and Disney products.

Westpoint Stevens
Call 800 533 8229 or visit
www.martex.com for a retailer
near you.
Wide range of linens, including
Star Wars products.

FABRICS

Calico Corners
Call 800 213 6366 or visit
www.calicocorners.com for
a retailer near you.
Wide range of fabric.

Kravet Fabrics Inc.
225 Central Avenue S.
Bethpage, NY 11714
800 648 5728
www.kravet.com
Variety of textures including
chenille, woven, and multi-
purpose fabrics.

Laura Ashley
Call 800 367 2000 or visit
www.laura-ashley.com for a
retailer near you.
Floral, striped, checked, and
solid cottons in a range of
colors.

Waverly
Call 800 432 5881 or visit
www.decoratewaverly.com
for a retailer near you.
Fabrics, wallpaper, carpets,
blinds, accessories, and baby
furnishings.

PAINTS

Crayola Paints
Call 800 344 0400 or visit
www.benjaminmoore.com
for a retailer near you.
150 colors of washable latex
paint, including glitter, glow in the
dark, and chalkboard varieties.

**The Old Fashioned Milk
  Paint Co., Inc.**
436 Main Street
P.O. Box 222
Groton, MA 01450
978 448 6336
www.milkpaint.com
Non-fade colors made to a
traditional milk paint recipe.

Ralph Lauren Paint Collection
Walls Alive
1328-17 Avenue SW
Calgary, Alberta T2T OC3
403 244 8931
www.wallsalive.com/lauren.html
Bold colors for the home.

BATHROOMS

Bed, Bath & Beyond
620 6th Avenue
New York, NY 10011
800 GO BEYOND
www.bedbathandbeyond.com
Modern bathroom accessories.

The Bumblebee Bush
www.thebumblebeebush.com
Online merchant of children's
items.

Smart-Babies.com
P.O. Box 530374
Henderson, NV 89053-0374
877 310 6647
www.smart-babies.com
Bath toys.

ACCESSORIES

babygear.com
New York, NY
877 302 BABY
www.babygear.com
Baby superstore.

Bell Sports, Inc.
Call 800 456 BELL or visit
www.bellbikehelmets.com
for a retailer near you.
Bike helmets.

ChildSecure
10660 Pine Haven
N. Bethesda, MD 20852
800 450 6530
Safety guidance and
childproofing.

Claire's Stores Inc.
Call 800 CLAIRES or visit
www.claires.com for
a retailer near you.
Mall-based retailer of preteen
and teen accessories, costume
jewelry and apparel.

dELiAs
Natick Mall
1245 Worcester Street
Suite 2416
Natick, MA 01760
508 647 9357
www.delias.com
Accessories, outerwear,
sleepware, roomware, shoes.

The Old Dude
P.O. Box 701
Lake Villa, IL 60046
847 356 2902
www.groovylavalamps.com
Lava lamps.

Silver Superstore
204 E. Main Street
Auburn, WA 98002
800 426 3057
www.silversuperstore.com
Flatware for babies and
children.

Swings N' Things
23052 Lake Forest Drive
Laguna Hills, CA 92653
949 770 7799
www.swingsnthingsca.com
Manufacturer of premium-
quality residential playground
equipment.

Urban Outfitters
3111 Main Street N.W.
Washington, D.C.
202 342 1012
www.urbanoutfitters.com
Kitsch accessories, including
funky shower curtains and
sparkly lamps.

credits

Key: ph = photographer, a = above, b = below, r =r ight, l = left, c = center. Photography by Debi Treloar unless otherwise stated.

Endpapers & **1** ph Caroline Arber/G-rumpy bear by Jane Wellman, cushions by Caroline Zoob; **2–3** Vincent & Frieda Plasschaert's house in Brugge, Belgium; **4l** Architect Simon Colebrook's home in London; **4a** Imogen Chappel's home in Suffolk; **5** Clare and David Mannix-Andrews' house, Hove, East Sussex; **6–7** Imogen Chappel's home in Suffolk; **8l** ph Christopher Drake/Diane Bauer's house near Cotignac; **8r** An apartment in London by Malin Iovino Design; **9** Kate and Dominic Ash's home in London; **10l** ph Caroline Arber/Caroline Zoob; **10r** ph Caroline Arber/Emma Bowman Interior Design; **11** Victoria Andreae's house in London; **12l** Clare and David Mannix-Andrews' house, Hove, East Sussex; **12r** Ab Rogers & Sophie Braimbridge's House, London, designed by Richard Rogers for his mother. Furniture design by KRD–Kitchen Rogers Design; **13** Vincent & Frieda Plasschaert's house in Brugge, Belgium; **14** Kate and Dominic Ash's home in London; **15l** Designed by Sage Wimer Coombe Architects, New York; **16–17** Cristine Tholstrup Hermansen and Helge Drenck's house in Copenhagen; **18** Michele Johnson's house in London designed by Nico Rensch Architeam; **19a** House by Knott Architects in London; **19b** The Boyes' home in London designed by Circus Architects; **20l** New build house in Notting Hill designed by Seth Stein Architects; **20r** Cristine Tholstrup Hermansen and Helge Drenck's house in Copenhagen; **21** Architect Simon Colebrook's home in London; **22–23** Sera Hersham-Loftus' house in London; **24b** Kristiina Ratia and Jeff Gocke's family home in Norwalk, Connecticut; **24a** Sudi Pigott's house in London; **25a** Victoria Andreae's house in London; **25b** Kate and Dominic Ash's home in London; **26l** Family home, Bankside, London; **26r** & **27** Sudi Pigott's house in London; **28a** Julia & David O'Driscoll's house in London; **28b** Belén Moneo & Jeff Brock's apartment in New York designed by Moneo Brock Studio; **29** ph Caroline Arber/Emma Bowman Interior Design—cushion Caroline Zoob, quilt Housepoints; **30–31** Eben & Nica Cooper's bedroom, the Cooper family playroom; **31r** Ben Johns & Deb Waterman Johns' house in Georgetown; **32–33** An apartment in New York designed by Steven Learner Studio; **33a** Ian Hogarth's family home; **33b** New build house in Notting Hill designed by Seth Stein Architects; **34b** ph Caroline Arber/Sharland & Lewis, rabbit from Lizzie's; 34a Pear Tree Cottage, Somerset, mural by Bruce Munro; **35** Sue & Lars-Christian Brask's house in London designed by Susie Atkinson Design; **36al** Suzanne & Christopher Sharp's house in London; **36bl** The Boyes' home in London designed by Circus Architects; **36br** Sarah Munro and Brian Ayling's home in London; **37l** Wim and Josephine's apartment in Amsterdam; **37ar** ph Christopher Drake/Marisa Cavalli's home in Milan; **37br** Catherine Chermayeff & Jonathan David's family home in New York, designed by Asfour Guzy Architects; **38–39** David & Macerena Wheldon's house in London designed by Fiona McLean; **40l** An apartment in London by Malin Iovino Design; **40r** Family home, Bankside, London; **41l** A family home in Manhattan, designed by architect Amanda Martocchio and Gustavo Martinez Design; **42** A family home in London; **43l** Architect Simon Colebrook's home in London; **43r** Cristine Tholstrup Hermansen and Helge Drenck's house in Copenhagen; **44l** Ian Hogarth's family home; **44r** Belén Moneo & Jeff Brock's apartment in New York designed by Moneo Brock Studio; **45l** ph Caroline Arber/artist Jessica Zoob's family home in London, chair and table from Housepoints; **46a** ph Caroline Arber; **46b** ph Caroline Arber/The Arbuthnott family's house near Cirencester designed by Nicholas Arbuthnott, interior design and fabrics by Vanessa Arbuthnott, eiderdown Sharland & Lewis, samplers Carla Marx; **46–47** Sarah Munro and Brian Ayling's home in London; **47ar** Ian Hogarth's family home; **48l** Designed by Sage Wimer Coombe Architects, New York; **48r** Catherine Chermayeff & Jonathan David's family home in New York, designed by Asfour Guzy Architects; **49** A family home in Manhattan, designed by architect Amanda Martocchio and Gustavo Martinez Design; **50** Kristiina Ratia and Jeff Gocke's family home in Norwalk, Connecticut; **51l** Family home, Bankside, London; **51r** Designed by Ash Sakula Architects; **52bl** Paul Balland and Jane Wadham of jwflowers.com's family home in London; **52r** A family home in London; **52ar** The Swedish Chair—Lena Renkel Eriksson; **53l** Designed by Sage Wimer Coombe Architects, New York; **53br** Architect Simon Colebrook's home in London; **54** Ben Johns & Deb Waterman Johns' house in Georgetown; **55** Robert Elms and Christina Wilson's family home in London; **56l** Vincent & Frieda Plasschaert's house in Brugge, Belgium; **56r** ph Caroline Arber/Hoggy & Mark Nicholl's home in Wiltshire, decorator John Nurmington, Malmesbury; **57b** Vincent & Frieda Plasschaert's house in Brugge, Belgium; **58al** Ben Johns & Deb Waterman Johns' house in Georgetown; **58bl** Paul Balland and Jane Wadham of jwflowers.com's family home in London; **58r** Fifth Avenue Residence, New York City designed by Bruce Bierman Design, Inc.; **59l** Sophie Eadie's home in London; **59br** Ab Rogers & Sophie Braimbridge's House, London, designed by Richard Rogers for his mother. Furniture design by KRD–Kitchen Rogers Design.

architects and designers whose work is featured in this book

Amanda Martocchio, Architect
189 Brushy Ridge Road
New Canaan, CT 06840
Pages **41l**, **49**.

Asfour Guzy Architects
212 334 9350
easfour@asfourguzy.com
Pages **37br**, **48r**.

Ash Sakula Architects
www.ashsak.com
Page **51r**.

Brian Ayling, Artist
+ 44 20 8802 9853
Pages **36br**, **46–47**.

Bruce Bierman Design, Inc.
www.biermandesign.com
Page **58r**.

Bruce Munro
Mural commissions
+ 44 1749 813 898
brucemunro@freenet.co.uk
Page **34a**.

Caroline Zoob
Textile artist and interior design
01273 479274 for commissions
Caroline Zoob's work is also
available at:
Housepoints
+ 44 20 7978 6445
Pages **1**, **10l**, **29**.

Christina Wilson, Interiors Stylist
christinawilson@btopenworld.com
Page **55**.

Circus Architects
+ 44 20 7953 7322
Pages **19b**, **36bl**.

Dive Architects
www.divearchitects.com
Pages **26l**, **40r**, **51l**.

Dominic Ash Ltd
tel/fax: + 44 20 7689 0676
dominic@dominicash.co.uk
Pages **9**, **14**, **25b**.

Emma Bowman Interior Design
+ 44 20 7622 2592
Emmabowman@yahoo.co.uk
Pages **10r**, **29**.

Fiona McLean, Architect
McLean Quinlan
+ 44 20 8767 1633
Pages **38–39**.

Gustavo Martinez Design
212 686 3102
gmdecor@aol.com
Pages **41l**, **49**.

Imogen Chappel
+ 44 7803 156081
Pages **6–7**.

Jane Wellman
A hand-crafter of teddy bears
+ 44 20 8275 0693
Page **1**.

Jessica Zoob
Artist
www.jessicazoob.com
Page **45**.

Josephine Macrander
Interior Designer
+ 31 20 6428100
Page **37l**.

jwflowers.com
www.jwflowers.com
Pages **52bl**, **58bl**.

Knott Architects
www.knottarchitects.co.uk
Page **19a**.

KRD—Kitchen Rogers Design
+ 44 20 8944 7088
ab@krd.demon.co,uk
Pages **12r**, **59br**.

Kristiina Ratia Designs
203 852 0027
Pages **24b**, **50**.

Littman Goddard Hogarth
www.lgh-architects.co.uk
Pages **33a**, **44l**, **47ar**.

Malin Iovino Design
+ 44 20 7252 3542
Iovino@btinternet.com
Pages **8r**, **40l**.

Marisa Tadiotto Cavalli
+ 39 02 36 51 14 49
marisacavalli@hotmail.com
Page **37ar**.

Moneo Brock Studio
www.moneobrock.com
Pages **28b**, **44r**.

Nico Rensch, Architeam
+ 44 7711 412898
Pages **18**, **42**, **52r**.

Sage Wimer Coombe Architects
212 226 9600
Pages **15l**, **48l**, **53l**.

Seth Stein, Architect
+ 44 20 8968 8581
Page **20l**, **33b**.

Sharland & Lewis
www.sharlandandlewis.com
Pages **34b**, **46b**.

**Architect Simon Colebrook of the
Douglas Stephen Partnership**
www.dspl.co.uk
Pages **21**, **43l**, **53br**.

Steven Learner Studio
www.stevenlearnerstudio.com
Pages **32–33**.

Susie Atkinson Design
+ 44 7768 814 134
Page **35**.

The Swedish Chair
www.theswedishchair.com
Page **52ar**.

Vanessa Arbuthnott
www.vanessaarbuthnott.co.uk
Page **46b**.

index